The Optimum Institute of Economic Empowerment, Inc. Presents

THE STOP AND FRISK HANDBOOK

Created/Edited by
Ryan Mack

Written by
Trinity and Travis Townsend, Esq

The Stop and Frisk Handbook

ISBN-10: 0985989009
ISBN-13: 978-0-9859890-0-2

Cover and Interior design by James Subramanian, Lit Diva, Inc.
Book Production by Joy Farrington, Lit Diva, Inc.
Editing by E. Claudette Freeman, E. Claudette Freeman Literary Services

Published by Optimum Institute for Empowerment
www.optimuminstitute.org

Ordering Information: Special discounts are available on quantity purchases by corporations, associations, and others. For details, contact Joy Farrington at 877-432-7386.

Orders by U.S. trade bookstores and wholesalers. Please contact Joy Farrington: Tel: 877-432-7386; Fax: 305-359-9200 or visit www.optimuminstitute.org.

Printed in the United States of America

DEDICATION

This book is dedicated to the Brothers and Sisters in the community striving everyday to make a better life.

ADDITIONAL BOOKS

Less Talk More Action edited by Ryan Mack

Living in the Village by Ryan Mack

When the Cops Come Knockin': Illustrated Guide to Criminal Law: Series by Travis and Trinity Townsend

TABLE OF CONTENTS

INTRODUCTION

THE PRIMARY PURPOSE of this handbook is to educate those in urban communities about their constitutional rights should they be stopped by a police officer. The "stop and frisk" strategy used by police is a growing trend nationally; and while many police officers have used this method with good intent, many in our communities have also been wrongfully profiled and harassed. Additionally, many detained using stop and frisk are victims of constitutional rights violations. A quick read of the material within this handbook will not take long; and will remind those who are most susceptible to being stopped and frisked of the best ways to avoid it, as well as the most responsible response to it.

The second purpose of this handbook is to promote positive relationships within our communities. This handbook is small enough to put in one's pocket and inexpensive enough for organizations to purchase multiple copies. We encourage organizations in urban communities such as: churches, nonprofit organizations, schools, and concerned citizens to purchase multiple copies and organize community walks to distribute the book to those who have the highest probability of being stopped and frisked. As the handbooks are being distributed we encourage those sharing the information to engage in conversation. Use this as an opportunity to ask those receiving the information about their ambitions and offer them resources that might help them become more productive with their time. This book can be an opportunity for the corporate world to merge with Main Street putting a book in the pocket of every person standing idle on the corner; as well as encouraging them to get off the corner and become more productive. It is also an opportunity for community organizations to demonstrate their willingness to reach out to others in the community.

The third purpose of this handbook is to demonstrate how tangible action can be created through unity. While politicians and the police department continue to debate the efficacy of the strategy, individuals are being harassed and need to be educated on how to most appropriately respond to stop and frisk. With this view in mind, I turned to the best attorneys in my network to compose the core of this handbook. While I created the concept, Travis and Trinity Townsend wrote the material, and now we need the community to help spread this message through a unified movement.

As a community-based non-profit organization, the Optimum Institute of Economic Empowerment will never stand idly by as community issues disrupt the capability of our citizens to be productive. One might wonder what "stop and frisk" has to do with economic empowerment. Whenever individuals are unemployed and not economically empowered, they are idle. With the help of the community, we want those who are most susceptible to being stopped and frisked to get off the corners and find ways to become productive members of society, helping our communities to become stronger and more viable economically. This handbook is certainly not a silver bullet, but I am confident it is a necessary step in the right direction.

Regards,
Ryan Mack,
President of The Optimum Institute
of Economic Empowerment

STOP AND FRISK

POLICE OFFICERS AND other law enforcement personnel may observe or encounter suspicious activity or situations while doing their jobs. When this happens, police are allowed to stop people they observe behaving suspiciously and lightly run their hands over the outside of their clothes to see if that person is carrying a weapon. This procedure is known as "stop and frisk." Stop and frisk serves two primary purposes. The first is to prevent possible crimes. The second is the protection of police offers who are trying to prevent crime. Whether stop and frisk actually works is debatable. Additionally, the stop and frisk practice creates the increased possibility of what is called profiling. This happens because a large number of individuals are approached under stop and frisk based on race and ethnic make-up. Because minorities experience stop and frisk by law enforcement in disproportionate or unequal numbers, the practice does a considerable amount of damage to positive relationship building between law enforcement and many of the citizens they are hired to protect.

The information now in your hands touches on the issues of race and ethnicity and their role in using stop and frisk. We will explore the circumstances under which law enforcement is allowed to stop and frisk individuals. We will consider what can be done to minimize the chances of being stopped and frisked. We will also give you advice about what to do if you find yourself stopped by the police; and where to turn if you feel that you have been stopped and frisked in violation of your Constitutional rights. Then we will explore the history of the legal foundation of the modern day rules of stop and frisk resulting from the landmark Supreme Court case, *Terry v. Ohio.* This will give you a fuller and better understanding of stop and frisk. The information wraps up with a brief explanation of what constitutes reasonable suspicion (and what does not).

When and Under What Circumstances are the Police Allowed to Stop and Frisk Individuals?

There are specific applications and rules that spell out the circumstances law enforcement is allowed to stop and frisk individuals. The police are allowed to stop and frisk individuals if they notice an individual:

- ☛ Running away from police without being chased,
- ☛ Acting strange, drunk, irate,
- ☛ Hanging out in an area where criminal activity is known to be common (this

is particularly problematic and will be discussed in more detail later),

- ☛ Exhibiting criminal behaviors like those of drug dealers, thieves, or others
- ☛ Looking around an area as if you are trying to see if the "coast is clear;" or if anyone might be watching,
- ☛ Moving around in a "sneaky" manner,
- ☛ Suddenly changing the way you are acting or what you are doing upon noticing the police,
- ☛ Being at a place at an odd time or wearing clothes out of place for the circumstances,
- ☛ Loitering (either alone or with a group.)

While this is not a complete list, it does provide an idea of the behaviors that reasonably arouse the suspicion of law enforcement. Once their reasonable suspicion is stirred up (to be explained later), the police are allowed to stop an individual briefly to investigate. The officer is also allowed to frisk the individual. If a police officer is alone during a stop and there are several individuals involved in the stop, he is likely to conduct a frisk of the individuals. If an individual is acting agitated or emotional, an officer is likely to frisk the individual. If an officer reasonably suspects that a suspect is about to commit a crime in which a weapon is commonly used, he may frisk the individual.

A frisk involves the "patting down" of the outer clothing of an individual. The purpose of the frisk is to uncover any weapons the person may have on them. Granted, while you may have never seen a gun, many people do carry them. Since this is true, it is justifiable (and legal) for a policeman who stops you to check and see if you do or do not have a weapon. A weapon can include a: knife, gun, stick or an item hidden from plain view that can be used as a weapon. Additionally, if an officer can detect from "plain feel" some type of contraband, such as drugs or other illegal materials, he is allowed to seize the evidence. It is important to understand that the officer does not have the right to seize anything that he cannot identify by "plain feel." For instance, it may be easier for an officer to claim that he detected what felt like a plastic packet of crystal meth shards; as opposed to claiming that he could tell by plain feel that a person possessed a small plastic packet of powdered cocaine in his front or back pants pocket.

How to Lower the Chance of Being Stopped and Frisked

The best way for an individual to avoid being stopped and frisked is to avoid standing out. Some behaviors will arouse the suspicions of law enforcement officers; so it is in the best interest of any individual who wishes to avoid a stop and frisk to also avoid doing any of the behaviors listed before. Your risk of being stopped and frisked is also lessened when you avoid being in or at certain places during odd hours.

Mind Your Movements

Police officers are trained to look for circumstances that seem out of place or that appear abnormal. Sneaky movements are considered abnormal. Creeping around or peeking into building windows while trying not to be seen; are all considered sneaky movements by law enforcement. Additionally, suddenly changing your behavior or the direction you are going when the police are spotted is viewed as abnormal. Acting belligerent, violent, or loud comes across as abnormal and interrupts or disturbs the quiet of a neighborhood. Running when the police are near or are approaching is abnormal. Doing any of these actions will raise the chance of being stopped and frisked and will give a police officer reasonable suspicion that will pass muster in court against you.

Be Responsible

If you drink alcohol, do so inside an establishment where it is permitted and stay there until you are sober enough to go to your next stop. Do not drink in the streets or appear to be drunk in public. The same goes for using drugs. The use of illicit drugs in any setting is against the law. So, if you smoke a little weed here or there, or pop a pill or two, you are already on the wrong side of the argument against stop and frisk. The presence or use of drugs is not going to help your case, or give power to the argument that you were stopped without cause. If you must get drunk or high, be responsible enough to stay inside and out of public view; for your own good. If you are found staggering or stumbling, closed-eyed, red-eyed, loud and shouting in public, you will spark a police officer's reasonable suspicion. An officer is always going to assume you have drugs on you if you are stumbling around or displaying symptoms of being high. Further, they will consider you a threat to public safety.

Mind Your Attire

Fair or not, your manner of dress may invite a police officer to stop and frisk. It could very well be that an officer can articulate how a person's style of clothing in a particular neighborhood is the same as the style of dress worn by people who are known to engage in, or have been arrested for criminal activity. For instance, if a gang is known for wearing certain colors or styles of clothing in a particular area, wearing the same styles or colors will certainly arouse the reasonable suspicion of law enforcement - especially if the individual is acting abnormally. Being mindful of one's surroundings and one's style of dress and behavior is absolutely important in not being chosen for stop and frisk. A person wearing all black and loitering around a bank or an electronics store at three in the morning, while looking around nervously, will certainly arouse the reasonable suspicion of the police. In fact, this kind of behavior makes it quite easy for an officer to explain why his suspicion was aroused.

On the other hand, a person wearing a suit and tie, looking straight ahead as he confidently enters a bank at three in the afternoon, is less likely to arouse the reasonable suspicion of law enforcement. It would be difficult in such a case for an officer to articulate any possible facts that would justify a claim of reasonable suspicion. Police officers have also created drug dealer profiles. These profiles can be based on previous arrests, popular culture which includes music, videos and movies with drug references and the clothes, shine and balling exhibited. If you dress, ball and shine like a drug dealer; you can present reasonable suspicion and encourage an officer to stop and frisk. Thus it is important that you NOT dress like your local D-boy hip-hop star.

Avoid "Hot" Areas if Possible

It is also recommended that you avoid high crime areas. Aside from obviously placing yourself in a position to become a victim of crime; you should also know that police officers conduct more stop and frisk practices in high crime areas. Now this recommendation may be easier said than done if you live, work or care for family in a high crime area. If this is the case, try your best to avoid loitering (hanging out for no reason) on corners and standing around without any direct business in the neighborhood. Have somewhere specific to go, handle your business and then return to your home, or travel out of the area quickly without hanging around or doing nothing.

What to Do When You are Stopped by the Police

In some cases, after doing all of the "right" things (acting as a law abiding citizen would, wearing neat and proper attire, staying out of areas where crime or suspicious activities take place, etc.), you may still find yourself being stopped by the police. What should you do if this is the case?

First, you should remember to always be respectful toward the officer. Address the law enforcement officer by their title such as officer or sheriff. Any show of disrespect toward the officer may escalate the situation. Make eye contact with the officer, but do not stare. Maintain a neutral expression. Do not slouch. Do not make any sudden movements and keep your hands at your sides. Do not run. If the officer asks you questions - answer them politely. You should ask the officer if you've done anything wrong. Do so politely, and do not become rude or angry even if the officer does not answer you. The officer may opt to continue asking you questions. You should answer basic questions such as: "What is your name, address and where are you going?" Do so by providing your full legal name (no nicknames), a single address for where you live and a simple one or two-word answer for where you are going. There is no need to explain why you are going wherever you are going. If you are a minor; you can give the name of your parents. Usually it is not a good idea to answer any questions beyond the basic ones.

If the officer continues to question you, respectfully ask if you are free to leave? If the officer allows it, say, "Thank you, Officer," and walk away. If the officer says that you are not free to leave, by law you are then under arrest (even if the officer does not say that you are) and you should remain silent. Tell the officer that you want to remain silent and would like to speak to an attorney. If you begin talking, or continue to answer questions after informing the officer that you would like to speak to an attorney, you are revoking (or giving up) your right to remain silent.

If you ask the officer if you are free to leave and he says nothing, you should say (respectfully), **"Officer, because you haven't responded to my question, I'm going to walk away now, unless you are ordering me to stay."** If the officer orders you to stay or physically stops you or gets in your way, you are under arrest and should invoke (or calmly declare) your right to remain silent and your right to an attorney by saying, "Since you have me under arrest, I respectfully invoke my right to remain silent and I request an attorney."

What to do if You Have Been Unfairly Stopped and Frisked

There are several avenues that you can take if you feel that you have been stopped and/or frisked in violation of your Fourth Amendment rights. In the event you are arrested and charged with a crime based on a stop and frisk, the first step you should take is hiring an attorney. Be sure to detail everything that happened during your stop and frisk for the lawyer who will handle your case. If you cannot afford an attorney and you have been arrested, you have the right to ask for a court-appointed attorney free of charge. Once you leave the scene, find a safe place to pull over and write down notes or record a voice note on your cell phone stating all the facts surrounding the incident. Important information to record is as follows:

1. The officer's name and badge number,
2. The exact location you were stopped,
3. How long you were stopped and questioned,
4. What the officer's stated reason for stopping you was;
5. What you were doing and wearing when you were stopped.

Your attorney can use this information for your criminal defense. Whether you are arrested and charged or not, if you believe your rights have been violated during a stop and frisk, you may contact one of these organizations to voice your concern and enlist assistance in obtaining justice:

- ☛ Local and national civil rights/liberties organizations:
  - ▸ American Civil Liberties Union: www.aclu.org
  - ▸ Amnesty International: www.amnestyusa.org
  - ▸ National Action Network: www.nationalactionnetwork.net
  - ▸ NAACP: www.naacp.org
  - ▸ National Urban League: www.nul.org

- Your local clergy (ministers, pastors and similar).
- Your local, state and national representatives.

The Problems with Stop and Frisk

Research conducted by the New York Civil Liberties Union shows that only 12% of the 684,330 people stopped in 2011 were arrested or received a summons; the remainder of those stopped were not charged. These numbers illustrate the inefficiency of stop and frisk and cut against arguments touting the effectiveness of the procedure in crime prevention. Even more striking is the percentage of Black and Latino individuals in New York who have been stopped and frisked—87% versus nine percent of Caucasian individuals.

Supporters of stop and frisk often point to a decline and/or a slowing pace in crime. But there is no true way to measure whether any reductions in crime or lessening of crime growth are because of stop and frisk. Other factors may be responsible; and stop and frisk likely plays a much smaller role than claimed by its supporters. The increased presence of police officers in high crime areas alone may be responsible for any decrease in criminal activity. It is also possible that improvements in emergency call response times are responsible. Improvements in crime prevention can be attributed to any number of other actions taken by NY law enforcement. Given the severity of the issues in question – 1) infringement on individual liberties and 2) the disparity in the implementation of the policy -

more evidence must be provided that the practice truly is effective.

Regardless of your position about the practicality, fairness and effectiveness of stop and frisk, there is no doubt that its use sparks controversy; especially when that use is targeted disproportionately against certain racial and ethnic groups. As a result, several civil rights and civil liberties organizations have taken up the cause hoping to pressure law enforcement to lessen the use of stop and frisk and to ensure its use does not disproportionately target certain minorities and ethnic groups.

Legal History of Stop and Frisk

The practice of stop and frisk has existed for as long as modern day law enforcement has existed. Generally, police officers have always stopped and questioned individuals they observed engaging in suspicious behavior or who merely "looked" suspicious. When circumstances warranted, they would also "pat down" the stopped individuals for weapons and/or contraband. The practice of stop and frisk, however, was not examined from a Constitutional rights standpoint until 1968. The landmark Supreme Court case, *Terry v. Ohio* established the modern day Constitutional guidelines for stop and frisk.

Terry v. Ohio involved a plain-clothes police officer named Martin McFadden who, while patrolling a certain area of Cleveland, Ohio, noticed two men exhibiting, in his view, suspicious behavior. Officer McFadden observed the two men taking turns going back and forth down a block, each intermittently staring into a store window, looking back and then returning to a corner where they would talk briefly. Eventually, a third man joined the two men on the corner and spoke with them briefly before leaving. The two men resumed alternately pacing back and forth, again looking into the store and then talking with one another.

Officer McFadden, according to his trial testimony, stated that he had been a policeman and a detective for over 30 years. He went on to recount that he'd been assigned to patrol for shoplifters and pickpockets in the particular area of downtown Cleveland where he observed the men. Officer McFadden further explained that based on his years of experience observing scenes as a police officer, the behavior and appearance of the men aroused his suspicion.

Suspecting that the two men might be surveying the store and the surrounding area in order to conduct a possible robbery or burglary, Officer McFadden approached the men. Court testimony said that by the time the officer approached the men, the third man was again on the scene. Identifying himself as a police officer, Officer McFadden asked their names. When the men "mumbled something" in response to his questions, Officer McFadden grabbed one of them (Terry) and patted down the outside of his clothing. The officer felt a gun in Terry's left breast pocket. Officer McFadden subsequently pat down the outer clothing of the other two men as well, finding a gun on one but no weapon or contraband on the other man. The two men were charged with carrying concealed weapons.

At their trial, the two charged individuals (the defendants) moved to have evidence of the seized weapons suppressed arguing that the search of their garments and the seizure of their weapons violated their Fourth Amendment rights to be free of unreasonable searches and seizures. The defendants' motion was denied. The court reasoned that, due to the men's suspicious behavior, Officer McFadden had the right to pat them down in order to protect himself. The trial court further reasoned that there was a difference between an investigatory "stop" and an arrest. It also asserted that there was a difference between a "frisk" and an all-out search.

Eventually, the case found its way to the Supreme Court of the United States. The Supreme Court found that while Officer McFadden's actions did indeed constitute a search and seizure of the two defendants, his actions did not constitute an "unreasonable" search and seizure. As a result, the Court found that there was no violation of the defendants' Fourth Amendment rights against unreasonable searches and seizures.

In the context of stop and frisk, the Court reasoned that several factors must be taken into account. One factor is effective crime prevention. Another factor is the protection of the officer. Ultimately, the Court held that Officer McFadden "had observed circumstances that would *reasonably* lead an experienced prudent policeman to *suspect* that [defendant Terry] was about to engage in a burglary or robbery." Such an observation, the Court reasoned, gave Officer McFadden the right to frisk the defendant in order to ensure his safety.

Reasonable Suspicion

Terry v. Ohio established the concept of "reasonable suspicion." Reasonable suspicion must be based on "specific and articulable facts" that would justify stopping, and if circumstances warrant, searching an individual believed to be involved in illegal activity.

Reasonable suspicion must be more than a mere hunch. It is not enough for a police officer to simply say that he had a "feeling" or a hunch that a crime was about to be committed. Reasonable suspicion is similar to, but less than probable cause. Probable cause can be thought of as evidence or facts that would lead any reasonable person to believe that a person has committed a crime. Reasonable suspicion involves articulable facts that would lead an experienced *policeman* to suspect that criminal activity might be afoot. In other words, the officer must be able to explain what things made him suspicious. So the difference between reasonable suspicion and probable cause is that probable cause would lead a reasonable person (who may not have any law enforcement experience) to believe that a person has committed a crime while reasonable suspicion accounts for a law officer's knowledge and experience in identifying and fighting crime.

Think back to the facts of *Terry v. Ohio*. It could be argued that a reasonable person might not think that the men were scoping out the store and immediate area in preparation of carrying out a robbery or burglary. On the other hand, a police officer with many years of experience observing criminal behavior may view the men's behavior as typical of individuals preparing to engage in robbery or burglary. Based on his experience, the officer can explain and express the particular behaviors that he observed that are common to people who are about to engage in criminal behavior. That, in a nutshell, is reasonable suspicion; and that suspicion must be present in order that a person can be stopped and frisked.

Race and Reasonable Suspicion

An individual's race or ethnicity cannot be used to justify a stop and frisk. The reality, however, is that some members of law enforcement engage in the practice of stopping and frisking individuals primarily because of their race or ethnicity. Often, these law enforcement officers will make up some specific and articulable facts to justify the stop and frisk *after* the procedure has occurred. Keep in mind, that reasonable suspicion must always precede the stop and frisk as it must be the *justification* for it.

In some cities, New York City for example, a far greater number of minorities are stopped and frisked than are non-minorities. This is probably because of bad or questionable efforts by law enforcement to concentrate and utilize the practice of stop and frisk in neighborhoods and areas that are populated predominantly by certain racial and ethnic groups. While many explanations and justifications have been put forth to justify this practice, it is clearly racial profiling.

The police may observe actual suspicious activity and are legally allowed to stop and frisk individuals observed engaging in that activity. Because the population in a certain area is overwhelmingly of a particular race, the police may claim that they are not engaging in racial profiling. They may claim to be simply stopping the people that populate the neighborhood. The race of the individuals is purely incidental. But when you do not conduct comparable practices in neighborhoods predominantly comprised of non-minorities the result is racial profiling. Racial profiling comes at the expense of the civil liberties of minorities.

Given the enormous racial and ethnic disparities in stop and frisk, the question naturally arises as to why law enforcement chooses to focus on neighborhoods populated predominantly by people of a particular race or ethnicity. The reason is driven by a belief that people of certain races or who belong to particular ethnic groups commit crimes at a higher rate than people of other races or ethnicities. Proponents of this way of thinking point to statistics that, on the surface, appear to provide evidence that show minorities are the primary perpetrators of particular crimes. The problem with relying on such statistics, however, is that they may not tell an accurate story. In fact, it may be self-fulfilling to assert that individuals of one racial group should be stopped and frisked at a greater frequency because they are arrested more often for committing certain crimes. For example, if African-Americans are stopped and frisked more often than Caucasians in a particular geographic area, of course

African-Americans will be arrested more often in that area. Additionally, the number of individuals in a particular racial group who are incarcerated is not a precise indicator of whether any racial group *commits* more crime. This is true primarily because several intervening factors play a role in determining whether the perpetrator of a crime is ultimately convicted and imprisoned. By way of example, African-Americans, while accounting for a lower number of overall arrests in the United States than Caucasians, make up the largest number of inmates by racial group in the United States. This means that somewhere in the process that begins with the commission of a crime, proceeds to arrest and prosecution, and ends with conviction and incarceration - Caucasians fare better. As a result, the statistics given to justify stopping and frisking African-Americans at a greater rate than Caucasians are skewed. Even if the statistics provided an accurate picture regarding the percentages of crimes committed by certain minority and ethnic groups, it would not nullify the illegality of using race or ethnicity as reasonable suspicion.

For more information and tips about police searches, seizures and criminal law, read: *When the Cops Come Knockin': An Illustrated Guide to Criminal Law.* You can find it on Amazon.com, www.torinitystore.com, or www.copscomeknockin.com. Your best weapon against unfair stop and frisk is knowledge of criminal procedure and your rights. Continue to educate yourself about criminal law and protect yourself.

ABOUT THE AUTHORS

BROTHERS AND CO-AUTHORS of *When The Cops Come Knockin': An Illustrative Guide to Criminal.* Travis Townsend, Jr. and Trinity Townsend were raised in the low-income, high-crime of Muskegon Heights, Michigan. They flirted from time to time with the wrong side of the law, but managed to escape the traps of a criminal record—by luck. It was in law school, as they learned the ins and outs of the law, that they realized just how many mistakes they'd made unknowingly—actions that could have landed them in the same traps that ensnared many of their friends. Their learning in law school combined with their life experiences growing up birthed a vision to empower low-income and less educated audiences with the knowledge to prevent legal problems in advance and to successfully navigate the legal process.

TRAVIS TOWNSEND, JR. attended the University of Michigan in Ann Arbor, where he earned his Bachelor of Arts degree in Psychology. After graduating, he remained in Ann Arbor to study law at the University of Michigan School of Law, receiving his Juris Doctor degree in May 2003. During his law school tenure, Travis served as executive notes editor of the Michigan Journal of Race & Law. Travis is now Managing Partner of the law firm of Townsend & Lockett, LLC in Atlanta, Georgia.

Outside of the professional arena, Travis is the President of the Urban League of Greater Atlanta Young Professionals, and also serves on the Board of Directors of the National Urban League's Atlanta Affiliate. Fully committed to making a difference in the lives of others, Travis is a frequent speaker at community events and conferences. Travis is also a proud member of Alpha Phi Alpha Fraternity, Inc. He is an active member of both the American Bar Association and the National Bar Association.

Trinity Townsend graduated from the University of Michigan in 1997 with a Bachelor's degree in Education. During his six-year career as a high school teacher in Michigan, Trinity leveraged his real-world street knowledge to make learning exciting. At this time he also served as a teacher's union collective bargaining representative and helped found and run a youth mentoring program in connection with the University of Michigan's Black Law Students Alliance.

This experience whetted Trinity's appetite to advocate for others through the legal system. He moved to Atlanta, Georgia to attend law school at the Emory University School of Law, and he earned his Juris Doctor degree to practice law in 2003. During his tenure at Emory, Trinity was honored with the School of Law Dean's Public Service Award and was a member of the Moot Court Society.

Now, Trinity is an attorney in the law firm of King & Spalding in Atlanta. Like his brother, Trinity makes time for community service. He volunteers with Big Brothers Big Sisters of Atlanta and has helped plan and organize King & Spalding's "Absolutely Incredible Kids" charitable program. He has also provided pro bono services representing clients in wrongful eviction mediation and has participated in Habitat for Humanity's Wills Project—drafting wills for elderly and low-income individuals. Trinity is a member of the Atlanta Bar Association and the Gate City Bar Association.

ABOUT THE PROGRAM CREATOR

President of The Optimum Institute of Economic Empowerment, Inc., Ryan Mack: Mr. Mack has a life mission to build and develop a durable financial empire geared towards educating his community and beyond. Ryan Mack graduated from the University of Michigan Business School (ranked number one in the country) with a concentration in Finance. His career in equity markets began in Detroit, Michigan as a stock trader and later as a trader for the largest NASDAQ trading firm in the nation, Knight Securities. Having a passion for teaching he established his own financial awareness group in 2003 where he began to publish regular newsletters about various financial related issues that were of interest to people from all income levels. In addition to being a financial advisor working with many prominent clients across the U.S., he charitably lends his support to inner-city communities by coordinating workshops and creating economic empowerment initiatives that teach the principles of understanding the power of financial literacy. Unions, churches, government-subsidized housing communities, municipal programs, non-profits, inner-city organizations, international communities and especially colleges and universities have benefited from the financial workshops/programs that he has developed and instructed through Optimum Capital Management.

As a renowned public speaker he has provided keynote presentations to organizations across the country such as Harvard University, Columbia University, Princeton University, NAACP, National Association of Real Estate Brokers, Housing Preservation and Development, National Urban League, National Aeronautics and Space Administration, National Black MBA Association, the **National Basketball Association**, **Microsoft Corporation, HSBC, KPMG, Johnson and Johnson, Six Flags**, and **Deutsche Bank**. With a strong sense of philanthropy he flew to South Africa to teach economic empowerment principles to those in need and has partnered with the local District Attorney's office to teach financial literacy to previously incarcerated community residents with the aim of lowering recidivism rates. He can be regularly viewed on television networks such as **GMTV, CNBC, CNN, Thomson Reuters, and BET** discussing economic/social issues that impact American citizens. Ryan has also authored his book "Living in the Village"; has been profiled in **Tavis Smiley's Covenant and Action** (a New York Times Bestseller);

co-authored a book with Kevin Powell entitled "**The Black Male Handbook**"; featured **in Black Enterprise, African American Family, The Source & NV Magazine**; contributes regularly to **Huffingtonpost.com, The Network Journal, Fortune, and Black Enterprise**; received the **Top 40 Under 40 Achievement Award** from **The Network Journal**; was inducted by **Medgar Evers College** (where he currently serves as member of the board) into its national honor society **PI ETA KAPPA** as a honorary member; and received **Tom Joyner's "Hardest Working Financial Advisor Award"** because of his efforts to empower the community with the crucial life skills of financial literacy. Whether he is counseling a group of doctors at a convention or in Rikers Island providing a free course Ryan Mack's comprehensive, exciting approach to teaching economic empowerment to all income levels has generated a level of much needed interest in a volatile economy.

Trinity Townsend, Jr., Ryan Mack, and
Travis Townsend (From left to right)

Made in United States
Orlando, FL
09 May 2022

17701118R00021